Respirator
BLUES

Respirator BLUES

Corona Virus Lowku

Elaine Parker Adams

LUMINARE PRESS
WWW.LUMINAREPRESS.COM

RESPIRATOR BLUES: Corona Virus Lowku
Copyright © 2024 by Elaine Parker Adams

All rights reserved. This book may not be reproduced, transmitted, or stored in whole or in part by any means, including graphic, electronic, or mechanical, without the express written consent of the publisher, except in the case of brief quotations embodied in critical articles and reviews.

Printed in the United States of America

Luminare Press
442 Charnelton St.
Eugene, OR 97401
www.luminarepress.com

LCCN: 2023919585
ISBN: 979-8-88679-402-1 (Paperback)
ISBN: 979-8-88679-403-8 (Ebook)

Dedicated to the victims and survivors of the
Pandemic Wonder Years

Table of Contents

Introduction | *xi*
Acknowledgments | *xiii*

BATTLE | 1

1. War
2. Aggression
3. Responsibility
4. Femme Fatale
5. Rumors
6. Downtown
7. Joke
8. Flight
9. Cruise
10. Mutants
11. Rebound
12. Strife
13. Gaming
14. Repeat
15. Feud

DEFENSE | 11

16. February 17, 2020
17. Fact
18. Control
19. Cleanse
20. Masks
21. Revelation

22. Big Shot
23. Intrusion
24. Stream
25. Rebuttal
26. Menu
27. Petroleum
28. Overheard
29. Orange
30. Agua

NEIGHBORHOOD | 21

31. Clouds
32. Concealed
33. Attire
34. Church
35. Kisses
36. Pizza Parlor
37. Patience
38. Retirement
39. Misery
40. Saxophone
41. Frozen
42. Contactless
43. Routine
44. Shopping
45. Mortgage

WORK/SCHOOL | 31

46. Workspace
47. Greetings

48. Non-Conformist
49. Delivery
50. Zoom
51. Social Media
52. Vacation
53. Teacher
54. Process
55. Home School
56. Classroom
57. Campus
58. Good Life
59. Prom
60. Missing

HOSPITAL/NURSING HOME | 41

61. Onset
62. First Responders
63. Emergency Room
64. Hero
65. Camera-ready
66. Booster
67. Bypass
68. Caregivers
69. Lockdown
70. Isolation
71. Sexy
72. Snack
73. Fever
74. Unwoke
75. Hospice

FINALE | 51

    76. Marsalis
    77. Rene
    78. Tina
    79. Emerald
    80. Slumber
    81. Hallelujah
    82. Sanctified
    83. Etude
    84. Jazz
    85. Empty
    86. Fear
    87. Funeral
    88. Rainbow
    89. Terminology
    90. Not Over

Other Books by Elaine Parker Adams | 61

Introduction

It was Mardi Gras time in New Orleans! My high school constructed viewing stands on the parade route and raised funds by offering parking, food, and decent toilets. I couldn't resist flying from Houston to New Orleans. Although the parking on the campus was convenient and safe, and the food was savory and plentiful, there were omens that dampened my enthusiasm. My son caught dozens of beads thrown into his fishnet; unfortunately, I caught one across the face that scratched my eyeglasses. The toilet was a major letdown, since it was an outdoor Porta-Potty, not a real bathroom. This year I couldn't sweet-talk my way into the school building.

Sunday night in my hotel room I began getting alarms in my head to get out of NOLA. As a New Orleans native, I obey my interior signals. I began lengthy negotiations with Southwest Airlines and was able to get my son and myself on the first flight to Houston in the morning. This flight is usually available, since no tourist gets up at 5 am on Monday in New Orleans. Months later I learned that the warnings were right—Scripps Research (July 29, 2021) released a study that revealed that "New Orleans' Mardi Gras festival of February 2020 appears to have driven one of the worst early outbreaks of COVID-19 in the United States."

The **Respirator Blues** collection expresses life for many of us during the pandemic. There are six chapters, each with fifteen poems. The chapters are Battle, Defense, Neighborhood, Work/School, Hospital/Nursing Home, and Finale. The visceral emphasis is in the chapters on the battle and defense of COVID. The authentic experience is the focus of the neighborhood, work, and school chapters. The vulnerable chapters are the hospital/nursing home chapter and the finale. The pandemic cost many of us dear relatives and friends. May God bless the victims and the survivors. We are still grieving and healing.

Acknowledgments

Early in the pandemic, beloved family and friends succumbed to the mysterious virus. This devastation created a vacuum in my heart that needed to be filled with poetry. Writing poetry had helped me though the flooding of my home and the lengthy evacuation caused by Hurricane Harvey. Soon after my first loss, I began writing about the COVID pandemic.

COVID Angels like Tina Bynum Green, my joyful cousin and family cheerleader; Ellis Marsalis, my super-cool high school band director and promoter of music for life and living; and Rene Rodriguez Soriano, literary giant of the Dominican Republic, mentor, and publisher of **Haiku Bouillabaisse**, my first lowku collection, guided me. Gratitude also goes to on-going encouragement and support from fellow poets like Teresa Church of Durham, NC who spurred me forward with a lovely note.

Finally, my family continued to challenge my thoughts and stimulate my writing. My husband, Andy, decided to join the family writers with his signboard messages posted on Facebook. My son, Al, many years ago fought a serious injury from an automobile accident by writing rhymes. He donned a tie with an arrow piercing a heart and declared himself a poet. My grandchildren, Aaliyah and Albert, provided the creative energy and exciting ideas from the new century.

BATTLE

1. **War**
   eyes look east look west
   search for foe destroying health
   buying gun won't help

2. **Aggression**
   uncovered sneezes
   virus catches ride to lungs
   COVID on the move

3. **Responsibility**
China denies guilt
no COVID labs or markets
blames the pigs and bats

4. **Femme Fatale**
East invades the West
virus dons exotic dress
pretty but deadly

5. **Rumors**
    COVID news stirs fear
    propaganda from the East
    mind and body games

6. **Downtown**
    clear the workers out
    let COVID roam the spaces
    declare surrender

7. **Joke**
   Corona comic
   unnoticed waits behind gate
   knock knock COVID here

8. **Flight**
   coughs and sneezes shared
   COVID—new plane passenger
   fear the middle seat

9. **Cruise**

   gets on ship to play
   quarantined in room for days
   better bar at home

10. **Mutants**

    crystal ball-gazing
    viral forecasts mystify
    new threat looms each day

11. **Rebound**
COVID's back again
two months since last encounter
next time shut door tight

12. **Strife**
Eris newcomer
variant spreads rapidly
sweet name bad outcome

Note: Eris is the Greek goddess of strife and discord. **Wikipedia**

13. **Gaming**
    routine spray and wipe
    germs laughing at the efforts
    troops are outnumbered

14. **Repeat**
    headaches sweat and cough
    folks say second time easy
    body disagrees

15. **Feud**
    spokespersons argue
    agency leaders debate
    struggle of egos

DEFENSE

16. **February 17, 2020**
N. O. Mardi Gras
declared a superspreader
grab flight flee city

17. **Fact**
COVID fables spread
raging fever straining lungs
just flu say doubters

18. Control
new rules stifle life
shut down schools bars and churches
go home lock the doors

19. Cleanse
bleach bottles crowd shelves
make special COVID cocktail
add olives for taste

20. **Masks**
   some defy the mask
   take risk ignore the warnings
   belittle experts

21. **Revelation**
   mask hides all the flaws
   bumps spots and the crooked smile
   eyes show the glory

22. Big Shot
vaccination time
formidable assault with
extra-long needle

23. Intrusion
jabs up nose in arms
eyes widen face grimaces
permission to faint

24. **Stream**
    home-bound COVID style
    body and mind imprisoned
    Netflix is in charge

25. **Rebuttal**
    quarantined at home
    neighbor now argues with self
    wins all his debates

26. **Menu**
no more eating out
diners and staff carry germs
public dangerous

27. **Petroleum**
band-aids slapped on wells
drilling now goes into arms
oil and gas bleed cash

28. **Overheard**
   neighbor may be down
   coughs and sneezes heard through wall
   not my business

29. **Orange**
   masks now in fashion
   fit for every season
   creepy Halloween

30. Agua
   let the spirit work
   holy water powerful
   sprinkle once a day

NEIGHBORHOOD

31. Clouds
   no more pretty fluff
   ugly forms hover above
   demons are watching

32. Concealed
   new look helps the crook
   mask covers face eyes menace
   hand grabs pocketbook

33. **Attire**
    pajamas clogs sweats
    bedroom-relaxed street fashion
    Corona dress-up

34. **Church**
    Pastor posts the rules
    no hugs or kisses allowed
    chill felt in the pews

35. **Kisses**
    kisses are taboo
    what's the use of having lips
    puckers go wasted

36. **Pizza Parlor**
    take out eat at home
    no dining in restaurant
    miss Stallone on wall

37. **Patience**
   doll ignored for years
   owner confined with COVID
   toy is new best friend

38. **Retirement**
   all alone in room
   community center closed
   tired of Solitaire

39. Misery
    no fun left in life
    party of one is boring
    dog won't even play

40. Saxophone
    COVID horn of choice
    whines out its unhappiness
    can't be left alone

41. Frozen
stuck in line for test
locked out of work without it
life on hold again

42. Contactless
food is left on porch
call-in order with credit
don't touch dirty cash

43. **Routine**
    dog-walkers on street
    everyone else indoors
    wish I had a dog

44. **Shopping**
    online buys look great
    at home clothes look wrong feel wrong
    too bad no returns

45. Mortgage
house prices go up
working from home builds demand
sellers own market

WORK/SCHOOL

46. **Workspace**
    downtown office closed
    new base is loud coffee shop
    features free wi-fi

47. **Greetings**
    no hugging allowed
    knock elbows or nod briefly
    mumble "hi" through mask

48. Non-Conformist
refuse to wear mask
take orders from nobody
first to get COVID

49. Delivery
no more waiting lines
hot pots but empty cafe
take-out rides a bike

50. **Zoom**
    business from home
    camera and mike in place
    phony wall background

51. **Social Media**
    mean banter online
    a lot of time for gossip
    somebody gets hurt

52. **Vacation**
    parent is laid off
    stays home watching kids and dog
    no pay hungry day

53. **Teacher**
    teacher gets smaller
    no bigger than a cell phone
    sometimes disappears

54. **Process**
>   teacher knows content
>   no one understands process
>   keep watching blank screen

55. **Home School**
>   stay-at-home lessons
>   teacher only on the screen
>   good time for a nap

56. Classroom
stiff desk is not missed
floor better for stretching out
Cheetos bag nearby

57. Campus
no smells from lunchroom
empty halls and idle balls
kids took spirit home

58. **Good Life**
    no school bus to catch
    roll out of bed into class
    shower skipped for days

59. **Prom**
    senior prom is zoomed
    sit at home in fancy dress
    DJ tries so hard

60. Missing

years of schooling lost
ignore the books miss the friends
mark learning absent

HOSPITAL/ NURSING HOME

61. **Onset**
    grim symptoms arrive
    fever chills aches loose bowels
    each one takes a turn

62. **First Responders**
    no back-up in sight
    cannibalizing work hours
    overworked numb brains

63. Emergency Room
cars now waiting rooms
full blast AC soothes fevers
sirens provide sound

64. Hero
exhausted doctor
saves a life every hour
earns a Marvel cape

65. **Camera-ready**
    grim ICU scene
    death is a tele-event
    anchor adjusts hair

66. **Booster**
    same arm re-booted
    change affects lymph nodes poorly
    not adventurous

67. **Bypass**
　　too old for virus
　　papers say no special care
　　skip COVID treatment

68. **Caregivers**
　　carers and cared-fors
　　raging disease spares no one
　　who cares for sick staff?

69. **Lockdown**
    admin halts contact
    all required to dine alone
    no reason to eat

70. **Isolation**
    elders quarantined
    peep at loved ones from windows
    safe from enemies

71. **Sexy**
    FEMA sends condoms
    baffles the nursing home staff
    wanted meds and masks

Note: **AARP Bulletin**, Dec. 2020, p. 12, Lori Porter reports FEMA condom shipment.

72. **Snack**
    popcorn for seniors
    housekeeper misplaced false teeth
    advice—"lick the salt"

73. **Fever**
     bowl of ice by bed
     trembling hand can't pick up cube
     drips a memory

74. **Unwoke**
     pandemic naptime
     brain in perpetual freeze
     wake up when over

75. Hospice

good to be at home
no respirator or tubes
so much love to share

FINALE

76. **Marsalis**
    respirator blues
    Jesus plays the piano
    Ellis heaven-bound

77. **Rene**
    frantic airport rush
    COVID on board already
    in the middle seat

78. Tina

cousin full of joy
lover of life and true friend
give her back COVID

79. Emerald

twinkle disappears
evil virus steals the light
green eyes fade to gray

80. **Slumber**
    COVID-driven dreams
    stalk seize and strangle the weak
    dismal reverie

81. **Hallelujah**
    Mother dies alone
    respirator hums and clicks
    mechanical choir

82. **Sanctified**
   deadly saint-maker
   unholy halo-giver
   gruesome soul-saver

83. **Etude**
   moaning violins
   soft and sweet sad and scary
   death plays the solo

84. **Jazz**
    COVID 19 scats
    omicron delta rhythms
    beat goes on and on

85. **Empty**
    dark room old man gone
    rolled to body storage room
    rests in the Big Chill

86. **Fear**
    hand clutches the mask
    undertaker sniffs danger
    COVID's in the air

87. **Funeral**
    casket closed no face
    mourners watch distant TV
    can't smell the flowers

88. **Rainbow**
    lose the somber black
    wear bright colors no neutrals
    second line must shine

89. **Terminology**
    expired passed away
    any words but dead and gone
    as if it mattered

90. Not Over

thought Covid finished
scrapped the masks hugged openly
news reports it's back

*Other Books by
Elaine Parker Adams*

The Reverend Peter W. Clark: Sweet Preacher and Steadfast Reformer

BLOOMINGTON, IN: WESTBOW PRESS, 2013.

The Rev. Peter W. Clark served the Methodist Episcopal Church during the latter 19th century and early 20th century. Starting out as a circuit rider, Clark later built and developed churches in black communities across Louisiana. He also held administrative roles in the Methodist Episcopal Church as Superintendent of City Missions in New Orleans in 1906 and as Presiding Elder (District Superintendent) of the Lake Charles District from 1907-1909.

The significance of this biography is that it covers the career assignments of a pioneer African American pastor in Louisiana. His story provides insight into the lives of other black churchmen during the post-Civil War period of Reconstruction and the dawning of a new century. An important feature reveals the impact of this churchwork on the family of a black pastor. Family members shared the pastor's heroic lifestyle, often enduring poverty, civil unrest, and natural disasters.

This book also discusses how the family, devastated by tuberculosis, evolved over generations. Four of Peter Clark's six children with Ada Clark died at a young age without heirs. One son, Lloyd, died at age 24, leaving behind three children, one of whom died in infancy. Only one child, Joseph, lived to old age, leaving behind one heir. Two of Lloyd's children became community leaders in New Orleans. Lloyd's son, Peter "Champ" Clark, was a pioneer black sportscaster, and his daughter, Grace Clark Parker, was a social studies expert for the Orleans Parish Schools. Their lives are described.

The book covers Clark's service from 1886 when he was admitted to the ministry, assigned as a first-year probationer to Macedonia M.E. Church in Clinton, LA to his last assignment from 1912-1914 as pastor of Warren M.E. Church in Lake Charles. There is a timeline of Clark's ministerial appointments. extensive footnotes, and a bibliography of related materials. The book is well-indexed. Special features include a selection of writings by the Rev. Peter Wellington Clark and a selection of poetry by his grandson, Peter "Champ" Clark.

This volume is a vital element of Methodist, Louisiana, and Black History. Selected as a 2013 Louisiana Notable Book, it is an inspirational guide for the clergymen of today. Clark was a leader trusted by the powerful and the small. During his career, he addressed everyday struggles, but also dealt with community crises as serious as nature's Mississippi River flooding and axe murders by a deranged human. Robert E. Jones, editor of the *Southwestern Christian Advocate* described Clark as "a good preacher, a safe man, and the men of his district are following him admirably." (p. 25)

Haiku Bouillabaisse.

Kingwood, TX: MediaIsla, 2017.

Like the marvelous seafood dish, *Haiku Bouillabaisse* offers a mélange of savory poetry. It is the author's first collection. There are 72 poems in the book which is divided into eight sections. Topics include youth/old age, good times/bad times, garden/yard, and the crises of September 11 and Hurricane Katrina.

Some of the poems follow traditional haiku format, focusing on themes of nature. For example, there is mention of plants like bamboo and holly and birds like nightingales and roosters. Many of the poems follow the pattern of lowku (senryu) and emphasize social issues. Some are gravely serious, while others are filled with sarcastic humor.

New Orleans dominates the lowku poems—churches, schools, hospitals, and, of course, food and pleasure. However, a book focused on New Orleans can't avoid reminiscence of the tragedy of Hurricane Katrina. The author presents memories of a happy and vivid past along with the mourning and coping that accompany the post-Katrina future. The September 11 poems remind us that we have grieved before.

The book is designed to share narratives about each poem. The intent is to draw an emotional response from the reader. Between each poem and narrative, there is space on the page for the reader to jot thoughts. The brevity of haiku encourages concentrated thought but may also trigger swift reaction. The poems should be relished like the rich tidbits in a bouillabaisse meal.

Hurricane Harvey Lowku

PARKER, CO: OUTSKIRTS PRESS, 2019.

Hurricane Harvey Lowku captures the author's experiences and observations as a hurricane victim. Her home was flooded because of the release of waters from local dams. Writing poetry provided a means of coping with the disaster. It offered a sense of control.

This collection of poems emphasizes lowku or senryu, a form of haiku that emphasizes social issues rather than nature. There are fifty poems divided evenly among five sections—risk, rescue, recovery, restoration, and return.

A special feature of the collection is that each poem is accompanied by a narrative containing useful knowledge about the hurricane and its flooding. Physical effects such as power outages, street "canals," and rodent flight are detailed.

Much of the collection describes human efforts to address the hurricane aftermath. The early days brought piles of trash and drowned plants. Evacuees crowded shelters and hotel rooms. FEMA created anxiety, but the city responded with the mantra "Houston Strong."

Hurricane Harvey Lowku is an informative mirror of events occurring across the country because of climate change. The data in the narratives are real and enlightening. The condensed format of lowku encourages thoughtful analysis on the part of both the reader and the writer.

www.ingramcontent.com/pod-product-compliance
Lightning Source LLC
LaVergne TN
LVHW051958060526
838201LV00059B/3720